Interrogation of Morning

Praise for *Interrogation of Morning*

Lisa C. Taylor's new book of poems, *Interrogation of Morning,* is a stellar marriage of close observation and an energetic imagination. Exploring what she calls 'Love's geometry' Taylor maps out a territory of beginnings and elegies, of questions and paradoxes. Three stunning poems remember her father; a self-portrait is fashioned from heady non sequiturs; and an evocative piece riffs off Robert Frost ('There are promises to keep so I write the word *promise* next to *key*.//Distance is a promise. The road is a promise. Your mouth is a key. Your hands are keys.') There are fine narratives here (one poem begins, 'My mother's ninety-year-old friend sang *New York, New York* from her nursing home bed with such zeal it set off the alarm ...') as well as poems that ride the rails of metaphor ('Sleep is a dock without a cleat hitch, a dory swaying.') The speaker of this book of changes is in the midst of a move to the wild lands of Colorado, and she asks, what do we save, what do we take with us from the old life, what should we value enough to transplant into the new ('a folded-over page of Roethke')? 'Nothing remains rooted for long' she writes in an evocative pantoum, 'The Ferry Crossing at Inishmore.' Everything is on the move here, though what we leave carries 'the imprint of arrival.' And once we emerge from hard times, 'How will any of us know/when it is safe to mingle/over a meal or bottle of wine?' Here is a book to celebrate, wherever you are!

– Annie Deppe

This newest collection creates and bravely explores the boundaries between predator and prey, between warning and transformation. Taylor's poems carve images from a chaotic world, whether in nature closely observed – a snail with feelers out 'propelled by hunch or hunger' – or in memories of a devoutly superstitious great-grandmother who 'buried sickness on a plate twenty-two steps from the back door' and believed 'tragedies elbowed past regardless of daily prayers.'

– David Morse

Opening *Interrogation of Morning*, the reader will discover a father missing a middle name and last words, a mother who shares her apartment with ants, and a child pedaling uphill 'out of earshot of growling voices/bisecting air.' This is also a book about nature, death, lies, and reality vs. fiction. Taylor's poems are both introspective and universal. In 'Yearnings, Covid Times' she writes, 'We wait for a hand to/give the all clear,/not prayer or a summoning,/more like the gull with a wing trapped/under a piece of driftwood/that we saw freed/by a little girl/in a pink bathing suit.'

– Lori Desrosiers

Lisa C. Taylor

Interrogation of Morning

Interrogation of Morning

is published in 2022 by
ARLEN HOUSE
42 Grange Abbey Road
Baldoyle
Dublin D13 A0F3
Ireland
Email: arlenhouse@gmail.com
arlenhouse.ie

ISBN 978–1–85132–274–9, paperback

International distribution
SYRACUSE UNIVERSITY PRESS
621 Skytop Road, Suite 110
Syracuse
New York 13244–5290
USA
Email: supress@syr.edu
www.syracuseuniversitypress.syr.edu

© Lisa C Taylor, 2022

The moral right of the author has been asserted

Typesetting by Arlen House

cover images by Justin Q Taylor
are reproduced courtesy of the artist

Contents

For Ames,
the best reason for hope

In memory of A.D.

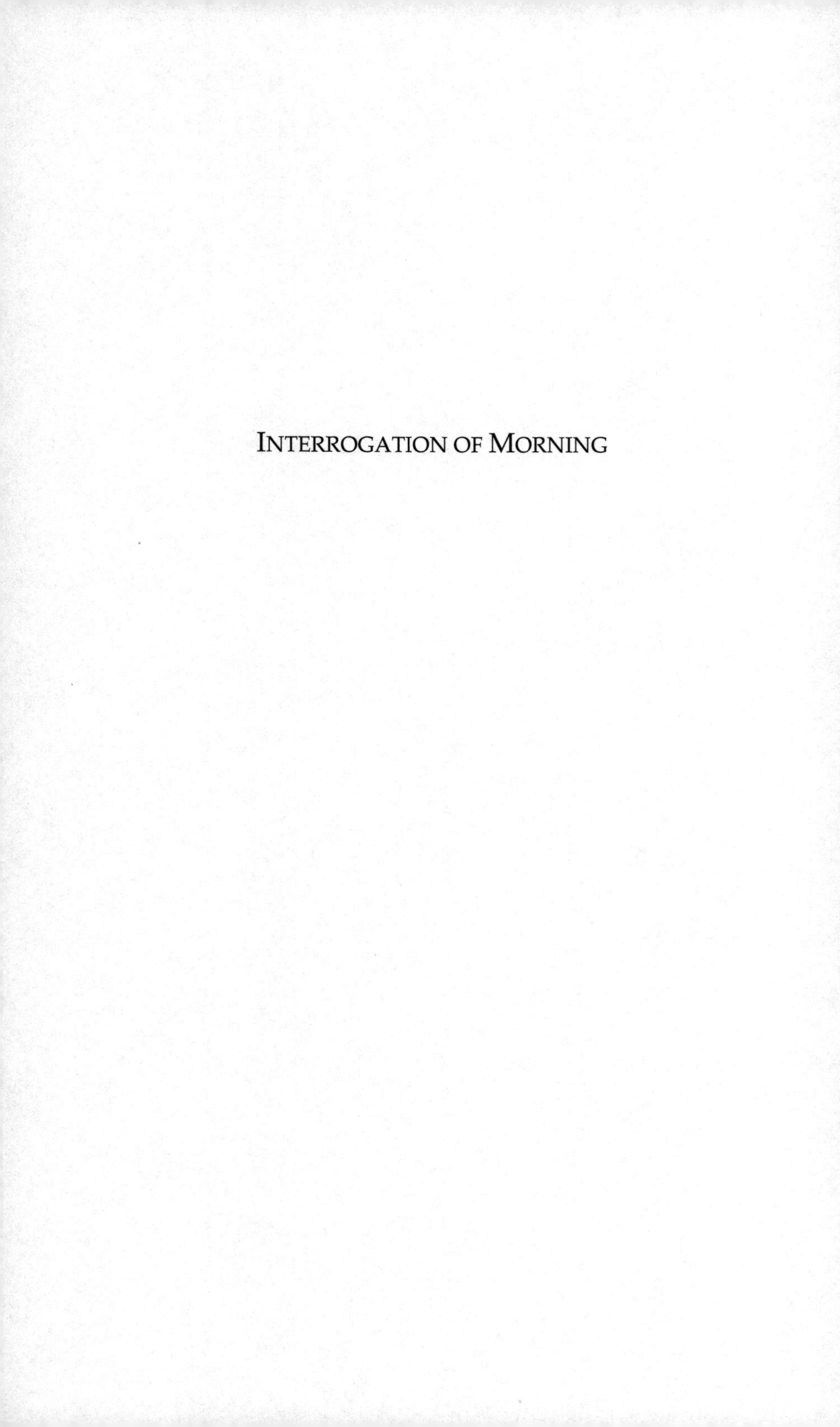

INTERROGATION OF MORNING

Mathematics and Language

Four magpies huddle,
black tail feathers twitching
as they alight on Balsam fir,
forage for remnants.

A stranger driving past
might see a dusting of snow,
pinecones spaced randomly
like ornaments.

How will any of us know
when it is safe to mingle
over a meal or bottle of wine?
Is there an equation for kindness,
a formula for equity?

The cure for loneliness
is kinship, a fractal
carried in memory,
tone of voice.
Love's geometry, distance
and relative position.

Your night, my day.
My hand, your thigh.

No one would blame us for marrying voices
or inventing language
without touch.

We are tethered to this morning,
watching the birds
and their tiny conquests,
our bodies humming and poised.

Counting Change When the World Ends

How you do anything is how you do everything – Zen Proverb

A wasp burrowed in a plum
sucks out sweetness.
Whisper of wasp remains
in the woman eating the plum.
She tests the skin of peaches,
pinches a baby's cheeks.

At twelve, I thought of death as a time-out,
a way to sink through the floor of existence
after dropping chocolate milk in the lunchroom,
Jackson Pollacking white linoleum
with blood-like spatters: life as crime scene.
I wasn't really there, no Ma'am.
I was counting change or pulling up socks,
scanning tables for a possible seat.

When I ingest, digest, I take in matter and transform it
to breathe and live.
Is it madness to imagine molecules, marrow, blood,
disintegration, and all that I won't write
about the slow death of everything?

I never dropped chocolate milk
but I've been mortified at school
and I once ate a fly.

It's a kind of forgiveness to acknowledge weakness
and mortality. The casing grows weary, night air
is bracing. Where have I seen this before?

How you do anything is how you do everything.

It took my mother till ninety to lose vanity,
though she enjoys polished nails
and coiffed hair. Hiding broken capillaries
and wrinkles denies age its due.

This is what a closing sky looks like.

Cruelties shuffle in line, carry
a perfect piece of fruit ruined
by tiny perforations. Curiosity pricked
by conformity spreads fantastical stories,
like the one about the wasp that may
or may not be true.

The woman walking by in a dress I donated
landed a job, and she could now pay her rent,
buy boots for winter. That's a story
I tell myself.

Death leaves behind cardigans, good dress shoes,
silk scarves for others to wear.

The life of discarded stuff is as secret
as the contents of packages
I mail to people
who might need them.
Sometimes I get it wrong but remember,

I once ate a fly. I don't always know
what we need to survive.

Grace

Sometimes I awaken and cannot breathe,
the country freefalling
from skyscrapers and redwoods,
people smudged,
then just crisscrossed lines.

For months I've been discovering signs,
ice that sheathes a leaf,
clefts of fire in nimbus and stratus.
Everything seems broken and frost
struggles to cover grit and stones.

The moment my foot found the ledge,
and I floated instead of sinking,
I looked out at a royal span dotted
with geese and brushstroke clouds,
heard the counterpoint
of honk and wind.

I pull on fleece and boots
against the buffet of cold,
and I'm six again,
dragging the frayed rope
of my Flexible Flyer across the street,
hush and scrape of runners.

A spruce genuflects
in a snowy field
and branches feather
across the map of the remade world,

a world
still holding its breath.

Imposter

Shadows of buildings inhaled exhaust
as I counted my remaining freedoms,
invoked gods
while your fever rose.

We sang *Amazing Grace*
to the walk light and fire hydrant.

Night is a thief, you said.

Streetlights beckoned.
We wandered into a part of town
with shelter for the healthy poor.
You handed the girl with a headscarf
your woollen coat.

The night after
you stopped breathing,
the moon was bloated.
Only a handful of stars showed up.

I spun into a city I did not know,
opened doors to meet sisters, uncles,
foreign friends,
tentative and visible.

I called you the name you chose,
as if you would answer,
but your family
repeated the name you shed,

like the coat you no longer needed
because you were warm enough

and that girl, the one
with the headscarf
was shivering.

Lies

Lies save lives. The one I told
while hitchhiking
prevented rape or worse,
but I did not leash it and bring it home,
thanking instead the gods
of imagination.

If you lie enough,
brain waves habituate
and you may believe
your own fabrication.

A writer once labelled his bestselling
novel, *memoir*, but truth swelled
like a gnat bite,
infected by talk shows
and newspapers. Many

reinvent themselves,
hide the relative who died of an overdose,
change gender or religion,
like Jews and Catholics did
to avoid genocide.

My little untruths
wag their tails, and I scratch them
behind the ears, promise to do better,
keep them innocuous and invisible.

In a literal world of horror,
Facebook, Instagram
and TikTok surgically alter
facts, bodies and faces.

When you tell the truth
you may lose elections, get
passed over for promotion, retire poor
and disillusioned. You see
someone else's face in the mirror.

Addictive and risky
lies are like a *deepfake,*
a term learned
from a student:
to manipulate or generate content
with an intent to deceive.
Riots become a tourist event,
pundits tout cures that may harm
or at best, do nothing.

The compartment of the unreal
is not representational
of any living thing.
Like a disclaimer in novels,
any resemblance to actual people, living
or dead, is purely coincidental.
This is a work of fiction,

this is a work of fiction.

November

will never be May
with its glimpse of green,
and indigo petals.
Not December

with a promise of glitter
and celebration. Who hasn't driven
through neighbourhoods
to see festooned houses?

November is a heart patient in surgery,
a Wednesday,
car stalled on the unpaved road
to the best beach.

Thirty days can seem eternal
when mornings crisp the grass, ice spangles
the windshield, and the sun
blinks shut by half four.

November is an empty cup,
starless night, patch of dirt.
November as unfinished love story,
trip delayed,
fever vision of a child.

When the edges of peonies curl,
and pansies lose colour,
the lavender is ready to be dried,
hung or sewn into cloth
to scent air or clothes
with summer's blue.

It's time to stare down darkness,
eat stew with potatoes,
look out closed windows.

Root vegetables
doze in baskets and wool blankets
shake out of storage. Quiet returns
like the best kind of friend,

one who knows better than to fill
every space with conversation,
pulls up an overstuffed chair,
and sips another cup of tea.

Unseasonable

No one has to convince me
that words matter. I've rewritten
my life story over a dozen times,
each time
with fewer antagonists
and more heroes.

Does the sky
have any right to incessant blue
and why do dogged leaves
hold on?
It is halfway
through a new year,
time to write lists,
conjure joy.

I'm carrying buoyancy
in one of those inside pockets
close to my heart,
safe from capricious weather.

Taking my cue
from this balmy day,
I foresee a turn
toward decency,

or failing that,
a blizzard.

Visualisation

She says, *envision your pain*
outside your body.
I put it in the shed
west of my property,
rough-shingled,
slightly askance shelter
teens discovered years ago,
then claimed for weekend parties,
their din stretched gauzy
over maples, to a row
of juniper,

by the old dog house
where my collie used to nap,
paws extended over the lip
of wood intended
to keep drizzle out
though water seeped
into the structure every spring,
swelling the roof with dark trails
of exposed nails.

The shed, better constructed,
welcomed an old mattress,
cans and bottles,
condom wrappers, hair ties,
and a blue candle in a jelly jar,
matches left for the next person
to smoke something
or drop at the edge of winter
when dryness becomes its own season

and yellow-orange fire
snaps and blazes,

like manufactured stars
falling up,
before fizzling,

pain now skittering
across the frozen ground.

Wilderness Doesn't Require my Assistance

I strive to be brave
when confronting the unknown,
thicket on both sides,
leather sheen of a spider
with a crimson hourglass
on its underbelly. On the trail,
I hear stirrings of a beast
bigger than snake.

I'm the person to call
in a disaster,
my thirteen-year-old self
kicking in, stealthily efficient,
tamping down terror,
broken bowl, burned spaghetti.
I swept up pieces,

grew to nurture children,
locate flashlights and blankets, sit for hours
with people paralyzed by grief.
Lowering the temperature
is in my blood.

When I see huge prints
not from deer or raccoon,
unfamiliar scat,
I call up that hypervigilance.
I'm one storm or flood away
from being swept downstream,
my attachments superfluous
when lightning ignites dead trees.

In cleaning out the houses of loved ones,
I pause to read their thoughts in notebooks,

finger pressed flowers used as bookmarks,
and donate suits and hats
holding their scent.
Partitioning sadness is a way
to move forward, less diminished.

Backcountry is not a world
I understand, ragged breath
behind brush, careening
rocks. I can pull someone
out of the road, prepare for weather,
make soup or bread,
run errands for an ailing friend.

I'm ignorant of how to save myself
from a landscape
that does not need me.

Cliff Swallows

When swallows soar,
addling the blue,
they balance between veins of agate
and oyster-tinged clouds.

Everything seen is tainted
and spoken language volleys
between extraordinary and profane.

The homes of cliff swallows
embellish craggy outcroppings,
their compressed mud pellets
rising like tiny domes
as they huddle on tucked-away cliffs,
sagebrush and shadow mountains
in the background.

This ingenuity of nests
affords impromptu grottos
where birds cluster
in the ebb of light,

an inauguration of season,
or a coup de grâce.

Poem as Dreamer Requests Help

My dream played Radio Ga Ga,
the noise of news turning to clicks
and chirps of unintelligible melody.

Does your unconscious
invite you beyond the machinations
of a bully infomercial?

Help me finish this poem.
Your dream may be key
to its ending.

Do you dream of animals,
a leaping cougar or rescue pup
resembling Salvador Dali,
as you soar
above farmland divided
into hues dotted
with trucks and puddles?

I'm looking for an interval of calm,
leaves gone to colour, then landing
on the outstretched hands
of old trees.

I awaken outside the jangle,
sheets tangled
as I approach
this poem's penultimate line,

its agitation.

Repurposing

I hoarded colours
as a child,
mossy pebble,
beach glass
with its whisper of carelessness
and death,

kept in a mason jar,
maroon and amber fragments,
shards of crockery.

A pottery fragment
remembered the weight
of a birthday cake,
and violet-patterned cotton
caught in brush
altered itself to my growth,
becoming a dancer's dress.
With a lucky oblong,
I constructed a goblet.

Each part recounted
history beyond the scraps,
an unscathed whole.

As a child,
I mastered restoration.

Mythos

Cutting through the thicket,
I sculpt a path to the water.

Drained by drought,
the river holds traces
of former bounty.

In the current's chaos,
a form emerges.

I'm not frightened.
There are worse things.

I watch the reflection,
pretend it is something else.

When she comes into focus,
and I'm not sure if it's cloud cover
or her hair,
I know better than to name her.

It can take a long time
for something to emerge,
even after standing
up to one's knees in water
poised for a sign.

When I depart
the tributary will continue,
polishing stones, nourishing minnows,
my makeshift path
strangled by roots
and skunk cabbage.

I place one black rock
with a stripe of quartz on the bank,
press my sneakers into soft mud four times
before reaching the road,

I do not look back.

LEAVINGS, TRANSFORMATIONS

I

Construction rubble
rounded after snow,
mimics a mountain,

vision
as interpretation.
What is unlovely
transforms

the way leggings
shape to the shins
of the dark-eyed woman at the café

or a concert hall cups the notes
of the first cellist
in the string section.

II

Do old hands remember
their younger version?

She once had manicures,
ten pearlescence points
at the tips of moisturised fingers,

now papery gnarled hands
drop a piece of toast
on a plastic plate.

III

Every fir and juniper
welcomes beads
of drizzle,

like a server accessorising
with a flash of giant silver hoops,
sudden art.

IV

I chase after patterns,
the shadow of a foot
dangling from a sickbed,
furry jacket
of a bee worrying the screen.

Musk thistle and common tansy
marked for eradication
are salutations
in places where little grows.

Beauty questions whether an aesthetic
defined by age or climate
is pertinent.

Time and predilection
are doorways,

lost keys, mortality,
leavings that carry the imprint

of arrival.

Keepsakes

Each obstacle I climb
is a rung on the ladder
I built at six,
carving adversity
into the bark
of the backyard oak.
The furrows were keepsakes
of a future I scouted
in a present
of reproach and wallop.

My older self would be taller
than my sisters,
and though that part never happened,
I renamed towns and landmarks
until a pride of ownership
prevailed,

flickers of recognition,
lace curtains and poems,

an absence of rancor.

Aunt Vera

Two drunken men
braked on a grey Saturday,
missing inside handles
in the backseat
of their maroon Bel-Air.

I pressed against worn upholstery,
small animal inside my ribcage
hammering.

The man riding shotgun called me *Chickie,*
ogled my halter top, ripped denim shorts.
I nudged the boyfriend
whose name I now forget,
while the driver took a swig
from his Budweiser, veered toward the guardrail
on the Bass River Bridge.

Unclipped nails raked through thinning hair
and he punched the brake three times,
until we bounced,
empty beer can ricocheting
off a stop sign.

In someone else's voice
I shrieked, *over there!*
knuckles rapping on the closed window.
Aunt Vera's house!
Squeal of Chevy brakes
and another lurch into the seatback.
Aunt Vera, I yelled again,
squeezing the nameless boy's fingers hard enough
to stun him into silence.

And just like that, the door opened
and we were saved,
pat on my butt, and Budweiser cans raised
for the fucking good fortune
of finding old Aunt Vera.

We sprinted across
a field of chamomile and beach roses
in the middle of somewhere on Cape Cod,
an unfamiliar house before us,
the sun burning
a goddamn hole
through all that grey.

Non Sequiturs

I believe in bulbs transforming
into tulips, lost dogs
sniffing their way home.

Foxes who raid chicken coops
need nourishment too.

The colour of algae and lily pads
transports me to a lake
in a rowboat with rusted oarlocks.

When I sing, my voice projects across the sea.
When I dance, I am a hummingbird.

As a child, I thought my bicycle
could take me to Canada
if I peddled hard enough.

Things I'll never do: scuba dive,
parachute, stand too close to flames.
Things I'll likely do: bike
on a bumpy trail, make a meal
for a stranger, love with abandon.

Nature interrupts us with storms
or calm. We don't deserve its beauty.

I want to untie dogs waiting by pubs
or convenience stores.

Uncomfortable places:
MRI machines, doctor's waiting rooms,
benches outside courtrooms.

Fire is beautiful, until it isn't.
Also stunning and dangerous:
mountain lions, venomous snakes,

humans.

SWEPT CLEAN IN THE AIRINESS OF DEATH

My father had no middle name,
a fact that baffled me at seven
when I learned the middle names
of siblings and friends,

just Dan
or Daniel, a name
that pirouetted
between one or two syllables,
never falling out of fashion like Harold
or Irving. Every classroom had a Dan
or Danny, and still I know a few.

When he disappeared, his name
became the view
from houses I remember,
lilacs in childhood,
forsythia as adult, and now,
snow-capped mountains.
Six homes in his lifetime,
only one with a view of blossoms.
Man-made pond, patch of grass, a doghouse.

My father had no middle name
as if one name sufficed,
wooden handle,
metal hinge,
practical and long-lasting.

His brain bled out
without last words, only
what he might have sensed
when scenes merged:
an odour of turpentine and oils,

brown-tinged hedges, bare branches
or the white-haired gardener
on a ride-on mower
at the community he last called home.

All is swept clean in the airiness of death,
swirling chroma, mounds of snow,
the croon of Sarah Vaughan,
renderings of Klee
in a mottled palette,

inexorably muted,
my father's name,
an incantation.

Keys and Promises

after Robert Frost

My daughter used to run up to me and wrap her small arms around my neck. My son once laughed so hard that his entire body shook.

In the road: a raven feather, drenched log, discarded coffee cup. The woods, as Frost says, are *lovely, dark and deep.* Waterfalls tumble under flecked skies.

You look at me from across a room at weddings or down the aisle at a market. I take child-safe scissors, cut and paste these moments into an album. On back pages, I include brief but inconsolable tears of children, disease and lies, a moment when you spoke in anger and looked away.

The landscape carries the skeletal remains of rodents and birds, a wad of gum thrown from a school bus window, a key to somewhere I don't know. There's a river on both sides of the road. Deer nibble grass in the clearing by a fairy garden my children built. The key opens an unfamiliar door. There are promises to keep so I write the word *promise* next to *key*.

Distance is a promise. The road is a promise. Your mouth is a key. Your hands are keys. The scissors rest on the table. My daughter and son live in their own houses now. You look at me. Still you're looking at me.

Ants

Ants are taking over
my mother's apartment.
In studious lines
they drink the poison
I drizzle on cardboard squares,
as I tell my mother
about the queen
and nest,
the science of death.

She forgets,
steps on them,
crushes a defector
between thumb and forefinger.
They continue to propagate,
ignore the noxious solution.

I suggest she share her space.
They don't eat more
than crumbs she drops,
an open sugar packet
pilfered from a restaurant.

Early one morning
she calls me, furious.
They claimed the hallway
and living room,

plan expansion.

Wild Thing

I pedalled around the *S,*
airborne over a tender mud hump,
before landing in the brook,
with bellows of toads,
and dragonflies flitting in cursive.

Everything afire, the jewel-edged scab
on my knee, pollen parachuting
over violets, a dachshund sniffing rainbow oil
abutted by sand I dented repeatedly
with my tires.

Each rotation brought
an uphill freedom
taking me farther than permitted
beyond the muscular world of childhood,
out of earshot of growling voices
bisecting air,
the breezeway door groaning.

A straight-backed chair awaited me,
filtered light, a mosaic on my dinner plate,
and I bowed my head
mouthed the words to *Wild Thing,*
mossy syllables transmuted into prayer.

In carbon black
I ladder-climbed inside my bunk,
pulled bits of yarn and sticks
around me,
while moths gaudy as dahlias
dust-battered the screen.

My Father's Style

The cold awakened me. Not quite frost
but brisk enough to pull the duvet
up to my chin and remember my father's sweater,
cotton pieces in a pattern
that looked inside out, *the latest style*
he told me, *a Coogi from Australia,*
where locals no doubt wondered
why Americans paid dearly
for clashing patterns and messy threads.

In his eighties, my father posed,
wool beret, diamond stud earring,
fitted black jeans. Still trim, he shunned
rings but wore a fine watch,
looked directly into the lens
as if he'd live forever
or so I assumed, pretending
it was an error when I got the call
four years later.

A man who had his teeth whitened at eighty-two,
wore a weathered leather jacket,
strode through airports joking with security,
though it was pre-Covid 2005
and the biggest inconvenience
was removing shoes and belts.

I don't know how he would have fared
in subsequent years,
pandemic restrictions.
He survived wars, the Depression,
the loss of three businesses.

On this autumn morning,
I remember how he dozed on a Barcalounger
in that gaudy sweater in midday,
Dizzy Gillespie on the stereo,

half-smile on his face,
and one hand limp on the arm rest.

Corporeal Dreams

In shimmery tights,
Nureyev broke
the limitations of gravity,
soaring beyond
my eight-year-old comprehension.
I feared he'd never land.

Mesmerised, I sat next to my father
whose preferences ran
to smoky jazz clubs in Harlem,
not sitting on a maroon velvet seat
with tuxedoed ushers
and gleaming banisters.

I ran my hand over worn velvet,
memorised the deco columns,
while lights galloped
across the stage.
Nureyev as hawk, cormorant,
fast-moving storm.

Twitching and wriggling my toes
in too-tight patent-leather shoes
I wanted nothing more
than to learn how to release

my corporeal body.

Blueberry Pie

In my childhood,
pie came in a bakery box
held together with blue and white string
I could make into a cat's cradle.

Rolled-out flour and shortening came later
in a shabby apartment with peeling yellow paint.
While neighbours blasted Hendrix
and Joplin, you looked for marbling,
that ripple of richness
that would yield the flaky result.
Not too much sugar
on berries we picked
down a hilly path, dodging bumblebees
and deer droppings, our basket
near bursting.

We left half of them uncooked
and thickened the rest with a roux
of flour and water, a trick
learned from Nana.

Trust the process, you said
stepping back
after the lattice of crust
was slightly browned,
the berries sweet
with a low note of tart,
not quite yielding,

a tree swing
on a July afternoon.

Heirlooms

She darkened windows
to halt vertigo,
brewed broth from chicken necks
for migraines,
buried sickness on a plate
twenty-two steps from the back door.

Her hairnet
spun from spider webs.
Dust motes saved in a muslin bag.

Great-Grandma wore
an underskirt, high collar,
rollup stockings of flesh-hued cotton.
Lip swollen on one side. Loose teeth.
Rolling pin and arthritic hands.

Kin, not akin.

She bent religion, never believed
a dishwasher could purify,
or anyone but God predict a storm,
but tragedies elbowed past
regardless of daily prayers.

No flights or island cruises,
her life a daily parade
of ladles and dust rags.

A past from fifty years ago.
A past from yesterday
or the last hour.

Her joy at a butterfly or rainbow.
Nature and love won't die, she said.

I laugh when I break a cup,
tiptoe around pieces
of nothing-that-matters,
keen over poetry.

No jewels, only
a delicate lacing of wrinkles,
sharp clavicle
under a flowered housedress.

Scarcity of heirlooms
when she died,
chipped crystal glass,
tin thimble.

Nature: A Play in Three Acts

I

Hornets outnumber finches and doves.
They hide in mossy eaves,
swarm at street fairs
and on picnic tables, bottle of Coke,
chip 'n dip.

Transformed by yellowjackets,
a lark bunting
now an empty pocket of feathers
abandoned at the edge
of past-season peonies.

Mandibles working,
two nearby grasshoppers confer
under the sun's blinding circle.

II

At Chicken Creek,
turkey vultures devour
an elk carcass,
wingspans massive enough
to spatter triangular shadows
on a blot of pasture.

III

Overhead clouds form a question
before scattering to the ground
as rain.
Thistle, bindweed
proliferate, mutate
in fistfuls of hunger.

After the interval,
the unseen takes over,
stage left, sunlight dims,

the black curtain lowers.

Prey

At the trailhead, we tread on piney
sod. A scarlet tanager
alights, too fleet for a camera
but you squat to photograph a snail,
feelers out, propelled by hunch or hunger,
and I scrutinise a puffball,
its symmetrical vents, an extravagance.

Overhead, a hawk
dangles a squirming creature,
chipmunk, we guess, like the one
who darts on our deck each morning,
crouched on small haunches, gnawing
bits of seed we scatter for birds.
The hawk circles, before slipping
from our range of sight.

Predators carry off worm
or beetle, mouse or ladybug,
loss camouflaged by an awning of branches.

Startled by a runner,
we pull on masks,
tamp down fear, inhale
the heady fragrance
of honeysuckle.
Like the candy wrapper
we see crumpled
behind a butterfly bush,

we do not belong.

Design for the Chaotic World

The colour of the sea found
six meters below the surface:
blue recast as green,
then clear or murky.

Yarrow and aster hold court
near deserted beaches,
while northern gannets and gulls
swoop amid the spray,
foraging for sardines or crabs.

In mercurial skies
the wind heaves its mastery.
Mossy rocks obscure hazards.

A ministry of focus,
the goblin shark
and dragonfish hunt,
muffled churning,
surface tremors.

Loved ones taken by illness or storm
hover above a residue of ashes
strewn by sons or granddaughters.

Deep dive to the place
where rare lifeforms
flock: frill, or tentacle,
singularity of purpose,

a design for the chaotic world.

Astonishment

I breakfast on the rust of rocks,
whip of windwalker sage,
make art from taupe and saffron,
sweep of viridian and stone.

Terracotta dawn
reigns over peaks tinselled
with snow.
Tawny Crescent and Anise Swallowtail,
the shape of astonishment.

A small mammal crosses
in front of me, followed by another
and another. Plump, brown,
and surprising as hail,
marmot or prairie dog waddle
across a makeshift road
with no edges.

The sun, a balloon, inflates,
suspended in blue.

I am hinged to this place,
its bleeding dusks and arid days,
the way mountains prevail,
barring avalanche or eruption,
broken pieces reborn as scree
to clamber over,
a feast of tinge and mist.

Chink of Light

The shoulder of wall
you leaned against,
overhead sparrows twitching
in June drizzle,
grass rakishly long,
not a single daffodil,
at the time I thought
the scene cluttered,
your breath crated.

I inhaled, flooded my lungs
with flecks of pollen as you stacked wood,
addressed me by a nickname
that sounded like
an undergrowth of ferns.

A husk of clouds pushed the sky
into a muddy rectangle,
chink of light overhead.
Someone bumped a recycling bin
up a driveway.

While I can't remember
where we used to go
that seemed important,
on a walk today we saw an explosion
of quince blossoms
in a neighbour's yard,
before you pushed a dead possum
out of the road with a stick,

because *nothing*
deserves to be wounded
more than once.

Whales

When a whale dominates
the frame,
everything that isn't whale
disappears.

A whale
is a kind of hope,
not a platitude,
surfacing in white caps
concealing migrating tuna or salmon
on their journeys
to warmer waters.

The naturalist lifts binoculars
so a child can peek
at the mass
that hints at relativity,
while a tuna
follows a conscripted path
of truth or ritual.

Salmon boats
don't claim justice for their catch
but food is its own reward.

Anyone may be felled
by microscopic forces,

the opposite of whale.

SHORELINE, MID-WINTER

It's hard to tell the difference
between sky and sea today,
even a jagged line of snow
competes, horizon, liquid, solid
and something in between,
the way that darkness and light
compromise in mid-winter,
afternoon a murky version
of early morning,
the world becoming simpler,
a decision to wear galoshes
or splash whiskey
into a cup of tea.

Everything seems vague
and rare, a halo of mist, undertow,
and untouchable creatures
below the surface,
where once I ventured,
curious and unbroken.

Ferry Crossing at Inishmore

Nothing remains rooted for long
a shaft of sun, percussive rain,
the moving sea,
a widening where tide skims sand.

A shaft of sun, percussive rain,
the brindled clouds, a strand of blue
widening where tide skims sand,
pallor of dusk unfurls.

The brindled clouds, a strand of blue,
striations of bindweed rim a path
where the pallor of dusk unfurls.
A ferry muffled in its mooring.

Striations of bindweed rim a path,
a dialect of growing things.
A ferry muffled in its mooring,
clear notes and a noble refrain.

The dialect of growing things.
A ferry-crossing, the harbour's tongue,
clear notes and a noble refrain,
graphite glide of bank and salt.

A ferry-crossing, the harbour's tongue,
the moving sea,
graphite glide of bank and salt.
Nothing remains rooted for long.

Clear on Clear

Here in the sky, we're a family of strangers.
The next seat is occupied by memory
in a suit
sipping vodka over ice.
Clear on clear.

I'm a pine bough legend
on the map of the river below,
friction of pebbles in my pocket,
quartz and slate.

I distract myself
as the plane
dips its way to new climes,
history of water stored
in the muscles of clouds.

It's how I keep myself alive,
memorising the flat line of grey.

I can conjure bark without a tree,
hollow flowers that mimic swans.

When I descend:
flurry of plastic cups deposited in bags,
click and shuffle
for the final taxi to the gate,
I fumble for your number,

a tourist gulping air
in the long-ridged tunnel,

now a woman laughing.

The Rule of Threes

Three men on faux leather stools
lean into their beers,
their wide glasses
like women's mouths.

After two drinks,
a woman twirls her paper parasol
until it snaps.
Piece of crap,
she says,

leading one of the men
in a leather jacket with a chain dangling
almost to his belt
to buy her another

passion fruit concoction,
ferrying her across the river
of her past
to a Siddhartha-infused
enlightenment, papaya
and guava sunlight
distilled.

Then she opens the door,
which might be the future,
stumbles into city dark,
a razor moon above,
the pavement below
slick and broken

under three cockeyed
neon stars.

Refreshment

Outside the sidewalk café
a yellow warbler reads drops of rain,
uncovers the scent of beetles
with her beak.
She's foraging
for a mid-morning pick-me-up

while he waits for the barista
with a tattoo of a goatee on his chin
to plunk a dollop of frothed milk
on his single origin cappuccino
that he drinks standing up
like he did in Venezia
where he spent a semester
wandering around Piazza San Marco.

Mi scusi, he said to a leggy girl
in oversized sunglasses,
and asked directions to a place
he had no intention of going,
hoping she'd take him somewhere better.

It led to sex in her apartamento,
the two of them on her bed,
drinking vino, eating crusty bread and olives.
It didn't matter that his Italian
was as bad as her English.
Her tongue said, like that,
while his hands improvised a tarantella
on her breasts,
and he thought for five minutes,
or maybe a night, that it would be great
to marry someone

who couldn't speak his language,
which is something he would
think at twenty

like the yellow warbler
who, right now, is not communicating
with song but with bugs,
pressed into seven open beaks.

Assassin Clouds

A hawk circles
with the vantage point
of field, burnt-out trees
and rock faces.

Hail like twenty stilettos
high-steps on naked arms
under caped assassin clouds.

Small rodents scurry
while the hawk sky-sails,
a funnel of intent,
ground squirrel nabbed
before the sky closes,
flat as a lake,

as if nothing died,
and the only drama
is people moving rakes and shovels
into sheds,
checking window
and door latches.

How to Escape a Fire

Close the door.
Lie prone
or jump out the window.

Evacuated in January
we held hands, shivered in the firetruck
in plaid pajamas as the snow came down,
shafts of ice shimmering in the blue lights
of the police cruiser.

Later in a second-storey flat,
a man I'd now call a boy yelled *fire*
and banged on the door.
I grabbed my purse, turned off lights, *out of habit,*
drove nowhere, just away.

Our first purchase,
box of a house down the street
from a dive bar,
yard the size of a spread-out blanket,
shower-stall-sized porch
where we ate breakfast
on summer mornings.

Smoke detectors chirp from low batteries,
shriek when serious.
There is a kind of flame
no one sees. Earth smolders,
forests transform into spectral projections.
Yesterday, the sun dragged a turtle
toward oblivion,
and four days ago,
a small city dissolved into ash.

In drought, we welcome
an afternoon storm.
Firebolt, tender moisture, electric precipice.

Crouch low so flames
won't find you.
Check yourself off as safe.

Check yourself off.

Crumbs

It took ten minutes to soften the despair,
her eyes rheumy,
a smell of urine in the air

and I wonder if it's the lack of novelty
that permeates these eggshell walls,
residents circled in wheelchairs
around a nurse's station,
napping after supper.

I tell her stories about Rockport harbour,
an art gallery,
and she reminisces about the crow
perched on the balcony of her hotel room.
It charmed her with its persistence,
though really it was only looking
for crumbs.

I'm the lone visitor tonight.
Residents stare at nothing
or doze until someone wheels them
to a shared room,
narrow railed bed,

yet I know she'd choose this
over being alone,
the fear the gate would close

and she'd be left on the outside
with no one's number
to call.

Grief and Enormity

The way *vessel*
is enunciated
and *wail*
is both grief and enormity,
the *whale*
surfacing briefly
on its migration.

The bottom trawler casts a net,
scales like trapped mirrors,
flat eyes looking
in the wrong direction.

Sleep is a dock
without a cleat hitch,
a dory swaying.

The twitch of tail, ladder
of fins, inhuman breath
under wreckage,
a tangle of kelp.

The way *mortal* is both wound
and life, not *mere*
but damaged,
like bleached coral.

No one remembers
the spot where fins
pouched out of cheeks,

or how much time
was spent slipping in
and out of water.

The Truth about Hurricanes

When a hurricane
rips across blades of oyster grass
and beach rose, projectiles
of stinging sand hit faces.
Waves heave,
flash of metallic fish and seaweed.

If someone were to dip a pail
into the murky water,
remnants of bottles
and limpet slippers
would settle to the bottom.

Churning and taking,
debris and renewal,

streets scatter
with militia, a virus infects
air, and a uniformed knee
wrings the life out
of a father, a son.

Death is no deterrent
for those who sleep
with one eye open,
while others slumber
behind electrified fences,
security systems armed.

Anyone with a place to go
scrambles for shelter.

In a city somewhere
a girl with six braids

sits under an overhang,
a man sips Coke on a stoop,

and I don't want to write what happens next;
circular wounds
turning blue, then purple,
the man in a wheelchair
struck with a nightstick,
blood pooling on his forehead,
water bottles and clods of dirt
flying like rubber bullets,
air thick with an impenetrable haze.

Debris ravages walkways,
splinters patchwork concrete.
Overhead clouds smother the sun.

In a hurricane, the last place to be
is near a window, by trees,
or on a beach

where the unfettered wind
churns and moans,
an open mouth
of fury.

SHARD

In late summer, when water dries
to skinny rivulets
and heat turns the path to dust,
you photograph oak leaves,
trade plums for the turning pears
of autumn.

Rivers grow fainter
with each passing day,
and apples rot on the ground.

When the current stills,
we cease to talk
across the long wooden table.
I place greenhouse chrysanthemums
in a clear vase,
watch them brown

until nights seem unbearable
and outdoor wanderings
are flickers
followed by darkness.

In April,
uncertain of the return
of light,
I turn myself into a shard
at the bottom
of the river bed
and wait.

Death Meter

My mother's ninety-year-old friend
sang *New York, New York*
from her nursing home bed
with such zeal
it set off the alarm.

An aide with an island trill
warned her not to move vigorously
but we cheered her on
even as death crossed trousered legs,
sipped iced tea
from the corner of the room.

I was inconsolable
when my twelve-year-old friend
was plucked mid-flight,
but I expected the slow fade of my grandmother,
funeral followed by a buffet lunch,

not the young uncle who spun us
across the sound in a speed boat,
hair whipping
in our faces.

We tick off nights
with the persistent songs
of spring frogs, bellow of wind,
savagery of winter,
our death meter running.

This Town Has Practically No Crime

The boy with brown shaggy hair.
The boy following his father.
The boy of eight or nine,

holding an AR-15
with one small hand,
weapon dangling down,
father leaning toward him
to demonstrate how to grip it
with both hands.
Now it is tucked
under the boy's right arm,
pointing outward.

She watches from across the street
as the boy and the father
walk up three concrete steps,
one only half there,
as if an animal took a bite out of it.
They head into the house,
blue, modular, unremarkable.
She sees the boy with the assault rifle
walk into the house,
shut the door.

She walks to the next block
where an older woman
is pruning her roses,
a couple on the front porch
of a craftsman house
sip out of orange glazed mugs.

Three bicyclists pedal past,
one raising two fingers

in a universal greeting.
Four doors down is a restored Victorian
painted in rainbow colours,
each section a different hue,
Love emblazoned to the left of the door.
A grey-haired man with a ponytail
arranges rocks he's hauled in a wheelbarrow
around a pink Hollyhock.
He places them over a plastic sheet
laid down to prevent the takeover
of loosestrife and ragwort.

The boy with the shaggy hair lives
in an ordinary house.
He handled a weapon
she will never touch.
He is eight or nine.
She was told when she moved here
that this town has practically no crime.

No one locks their doors.

DISTRACTIONS

You don't need a wound
to know that blood moves
like a train
through the tunnels of your body.
You only need the will
and machinery
to pump and slide
until every part knows
what it has to do – contract, retreat,
plump up the buttress of muscle.

It's a way in which you lose
a little each day,
cells seeping and malleable.
On the surface your skin
remains taut, responsive,
eyes focused straight ahead.

Meanwhile the undertaker
is making arrangements
and your family
has chosen an urn
for your remains.

Interrogation of Morning

In love,
the one who enters is the one who leaves

but the one entered is filled,
carries the shape within,
heart, tongue, spoon

pinging,
her right palm,
his left breast,
breath-holding.

Sunlight zigzags
over sheets,
shadow, blood,
argument,

interrogation of morning,
a shape-shifting light,
not love
but its signature

trickle of denouement
on her thigh,
his hand lingering
on the doorknob before
departing.

Plastic Bag in the Shape of a Woman

spotted on a tuft of grass,
voluptuous clarity.

I braked,
gulped from my water bottle
before pedalling past.

At an exhibition once
I saw a woman
slathered in clay,
art or maybe
something

like dying,
body as a transition
to weightlessness.
Discarded casing,
inflated bag.

Mornings, I bicycle by mountains,
dodge grasshoppers, brush away
flies. My breath keeps pace
as legs pump,
climb hills, cross roads.

This glimpse of who I am,
a line drawing,
scabbard over muscle and vein,
lung balloons, heart pump,

an invitation
to disappear.

Woman at the Gym

wipes her face with the cloth
used to clean the machines,
swings meaty arms back and forth,
keys jangling from her neck.

Something my mother used to say
when she was angry:
wipe that smile off your face.

Thump of her footfall,
clang of keys, and thwack
of treadmills and elliptical trainers.
Now she's mouthing lyrics,
snapping her fingers.

I know her role isn't to wipe smiles
off faces or clean the machines.

Terrycloth rag in hand,
she strides into this poem
staring at my clumsy efforts
and pointing a finger –
look,
and I do,

rubbing my words
over and over
with her soiled towel.

Fire and Water

Everything you thought was real
you passed on to your children
until those truths
seemed made of cinders and soot.

Someone introduced
another version, not fanciful but grim,
accusatory, petty.

You are told to believe it,
though it kills
those you love or might love,
shopkeepers, doctors, fathers.

You have trouble sleeping,
can't block the moans.
Survival seems unfeasible.

The wounds are inconspicuous
but you feel them blister,
striking from the inside.

Like a fire that thins the forest,
you want to believe there is purpose
to the slaughter,
even as the throbbing persists
and the stream of water
falls far short
of its goal.

Lunar Eclipse

A shadow of wing crossed my field of vision.
Tuesday, night of the lunar eclipse,
I awakened, looked up.
Stars blinked themselves into oblivion.

Tuesday, night of the lunar eclipse,
I saw ghost tracks of cars.
Stars blinked themselves into oblivion.
A shadow of wing crossed my field of vision.

I saw ghost tracks of cars.
No one spoke or handed me a map.
A shadow of wing crossed my field of vision
as I stood at the window, looking out.

No one spoke or handed me a map.
The shortest day, light erased from every surface.
As I stood at the window, looking out,
a light snow began to fall.

The shortest day, light erased from every surface.
I awakened, looked up.
A light snow began to fall.
A shadow of a wing crossed my field of vision.

LATE NIGHT RIDE

You're passing
over the neighbour's house,
a bag of mulch by the garage,
next to a labradoodle's
chewed-up Frisbee.

Whatever force propels you
moves along
until you're down by the Fenton River,
brimming after days of rain,
frogs shrieking in unison

and this time you're not thinking
about poison ivy or ticks
as you float
above swampy dirt,
fiddleheads and pussy willows.

Next, a long stretch of rooftops,
some moss-covered, others with broken shingles,
until you reach the end of the road.
A feral cat narrows his eyes,
the air thick and humid.

The only light is a snip of moon
and stars that pulsate
as clouds heave their bulk
across the char of sky.
Soon you won't be able to see

the raccoon rummage through a trash bin,
pulling up his snout to challenge invisible foes.

As the town moves toward
the occupation of dawn,
you skim over what this is,

a warning
or a transformation.

Roses for a Pie

I let myself out of the house
by solving a word puzzle,
open a box wrapped in brown paper
hidden amid a blaze of daffodils.
I get back in by hopping
on one foot.

Crevices in mountains house people
I can't see with ordinary eyes. I leave them
morsels wrapped in pink tissue.
They thank me with green pebbles.

I apply for chef, dog trainer, gymnast,
first violinist, poet,
my feet too small for ballet.

In the next world, commerce will be roses for a pie,
quartz for a dozen eggs.

This is what I have to work with so I spackle over
the hard parts.

Tonight, the mountaintops
look like flocks of sheep.
I stay in,
watch a border collie
herd the hills.

Riding the Rails

I jellyfish through sliding doors
of a train bound somewhere,
past aerophobes and a man
strumming a ukulele.

No television or internet,
just thawed grey meals and unclaimed faces,
hours of rolling landscape with sleet
pocking the window.

In town after town,
I forget about the dying and the buried dead.

When we pull into a station,
my boots clap on the frozen ground
of a town the colour of chai and ash.
Someone lights a cigarette,
another offers a piece of Trident gum.

Across the street, a car has gone off
an embankment, and the gum-chewing man
says, *probably texting— some folks got no sense.*

I book a southern route,
pass people sharing casseroles and kisses,
cars stopped at flashing lights.
A woman in a baseball hat
upper-body dances in her Peugeot.

Windows on the train rattle
and my bed unfolds from the seat.
On the track, sparks mimic stars.

I know a quarter moon is present
behind clouds

as night pulls itself
into tomorrow's unknown station.

CHANCE AS MOTH DUST

Blossoms planted or wild
unfold in succession,
cycles interrupted
by indifferent rain
and its pale twin, drought.

Remnants of ghost sage
fringe dry dirt
under sketched clouds
and armoured beetles
encircle a hedge.

Even the sun, mostly tireless,
lurks behind stratus
or scorches in places
where the juniper cannot stretch
to height.

Chance as moth dust, tatting
of tarantula and mantis,
and summer's daylike nights,
tendrils that steward heat.

Lost

Today arrived on a familiar wagon
of bleary light,
scattered spiders, tunnels
of prairie dogs. Miles
from any coast,
the shriveled riverbeds
and dried-out paintbrush
are empty of any tide.

Once I saw a dorsal fin
at Herring Cove. Will I paddle again
on the bay, dip hands in green water?

Cheeks ballooned
to blow up a yellow raft,
we raced, splashed
and dangled our feet.

No more barefoot nights,
squalls of seabirds
or enchanted walking
through tide pools,
swim at your own risk

and I do, in dreams
adorned with seaweed bangles,
down a sand-swept road,
wooden steps to the water.

One day I will leave
sharks, jellyfish,
snakes, and picas
in their respective habitats,

grab onto a braid
of seagrass
and swing it wildly,
inhaling ground fog
until I'm found.

Everything Not Flowering is Grief

The irises fan out
like a welcome basket
next to blue columbine,
a gift lilac flown across the country.
I plant penstemon and peonies.

In a drought, watering restrictions
are tied to address. Even numbers
water only on even days.
I uncover dirt beside the mulch,
grit browning my fingernails.
A layer of parch persists
below the puddle I make with a hose.
Rain delivers a grey spell
to mountains,
barely licks the lips
of the valley.

Everything not flowering
is grief.

Beach erosion,
hurricanes and fires.
Hate graffiti
in bedroom towns.

The blooms respond
to my ministrations,
unfurling and greening
in arid dawn. This morning
a yarrow I left for dead
revived and a firework
of pink peonies decorate the walk. Perhaps

a shred of renewal is viable,
like a shoot I once saw pushing
through dried lava in Hawai'i, proof
that animals and plants sustain.

Trampled, the Russian sage
blossoms, even in crumbling soil
under unflagging sun.
I scoop and weed to the backdrop of wind,
and a neighbour's rescue dog yapping,

remember the shades
that brought me here,
aspen and sedum, new life,
no answers to the question
of how long.

REDUCTION

Not born
with knowledge
to carry me through storms
or disease, I do not know
what to save,

a fragment
from my first set of dishes,
broken child's comb,
folded-over page of Roethke's poetry.

Artifacts of deterioration
surface with each uprising.

I slip out of my skin and glide
through obstacles.

If I had anticipated
the reduction of everything
to water,
I might have loved less,
jettisoned more.

Ephemera

What we couldn't take with us:
the fort our children built
from discarded planks and cinderblocks
invisible behind boxwood,
twenty skeletal Christmas trees
including one that took hours to agree upon.
Our daughter wanted the six-foot Balsam,
our son, the bedraggled Douglas fir.

The first time you brought me flowers,
hidden behind your back,
you materialised them like a magic trick
by the stone wall,
grackles turning this way and that,
their sleek heads shining.

Days grow shorter and morning glories
fold onto themselves at night
like clenched fists.
Roses will return regardless of our absence,
following hyacinth and daffodil,
a bounty left for new occupants
who may present them to a lover
or mow them over.

We'll plant prairie zinnia,
lavender and sage,
mindful of what flourishes
in desert drought.

Before we left,
I tossed pennies and foreign coins
behind the old woodshed,

scattered my cache of beach glass and shells
past remnants of a sandbox,

purple canna lilies
gaping in the rearview mirror.

Temporary Endings

I turn the chatter of magpies
into cooing doves,
visualise an intact fir after
lightning divides it,
a blooming rose before beetles
devour petals.

Where my unconscious goes
I don't always follow,
impromptu words, typos
that fold into images,
the way language and life
confound me.

The russet smear of sky
opens like a glade dotted
with fuchsia, moments
unscripted, hills I tame with brakes.

I want every wound to heal, cruelty
to have a counterpoint
of kindness, but language
agitates as well as calms.

Inadequate and substantial,
the heft of what I say diminishes
in the first snap of cold.

I dream of atonement
for brittle verbs, recalcitrant nouns.
When I am spared,
it is temporary, my bones softening,
words sloughing off wind
bitter with January.

What will become
of deleted metaphors,
persistent afflictions,

my temporary endings?

Yearnings, Covid Times

We dipped into that gem of ocean,
maybe three clouds overhead,
a gleam of sand.
Bright scarves and beads of locals,
scarlet, burnish, aqua,
Anali with her turquoise embroidered blouse
and silver trinkets.
In Huatulco, the beach next to a café
where we shared a Negra Modelo on a picnic table,
I bought an apple carved of wood for a friend,
browsed galleries,

and it was effortless to leave
for Cabo or Puerto Vallarta.
Were they real, those arrivals, departures?
Days of bare faces, hands reaching
into a basket of warm tortilla chips,
the push to board the bus,
staticky voice of our guide
passing worn photo cards
of poisonous snakes and insects.

Our yearning for destination:
suspension bridges in Costa Rica,
catacombs in Rome, white domes
of Santorini, even the bitter odour
of a plane as it begins its ascent.

We wait for a hand to
give the all clear,
not prayer or a summoning,

more like the gull with a wing trapped
under a piece of driftwood

that we saw freed
by a little girl
in a pink bathing suit.
She lifted the good wing first,
then the other,
waved as it soared
out of sight.

Acknowledgements

Grateful acknowledgement is made to the following presses and journals where some of these poems first appeared, sometimes in an earlier form:

West Trade Review: 'Yearnings, Covid Times'
Talking River Review, 'My Father's Style'
Live Encounters: 'Design for a Chaotic World', 'The Rule of Threes', 'Implications', 'Non sequiturs, Lunar Eclipse'
Naugatuck Review: 'Swept Clean in the Airiness of Death'
Sky Island Journal: 'Mathematics and Language'
Hawai'i Pacific Review: 'Whales' (nominated for the 'Best of the Net' anthology)
Soul-Lit: 'Grace'
Lily Poetry Review: 'Imposter'
Quartz Literary: 'Refreshment'
Angel Rust: 'Plastic Bag in the Shape of a Woman', 'Cliff Swallows', 'How to Escape a Fire'
Bacopa Literary Review: 'Wild Thing'
Crannóg: 'Visualisation', 'Astonishment'
MER VOX: 'Heirlooms'
Washing Windows? Irish Women Write Poetry (Arlen House, 2017): 'Ferry Crossing at Inishmore'
Insufficient Thanks (Finishing Line Press, 2012): 'Clear on Clear' and 'Shoreline, Mid-Winter' first appeared in this chapbook.

Thanks to Margaret Gibson, Eastern Connecticut State University, and Dan Donaghy for including my poem, 'Mythos', in the virtual Green Poetry Café video as a part of her Poet Laureate Project in 2020. https://vimeo.com/526250730
Still River Writers and East-West Writers for their valuable critiques of many of these poems. Russ, first reader, and best possible life companion. Peggy and Lee Cloy at Willowtail Springs for an artist residency in June 2019 where some of these poems first took shape. Kira Taylor for listening and sharing a residency. Justin Taylor and Charlie Chase for

spending time closely reading my poems. Geraldine Mills for long friendship, creative sharing, and treasured time. Gratitude to Alan Hayes, Arlen House for the continued support.

About the Author

Lisa C. Taylor is a poet and fiction writer. Her poetry collections include *Necessary Silence* (Arlen House, 2013), *Insufficient Thanks* (Finishing Line Press, 2012), *The Other Side of Longing*, with Geraldine Mills (Arlen House, 2011), and *Talking to Trees* (Finishing Line Press, 2007). Her fiction collections include *Impossibly Small Spaces* (Arlen House, 2018) and *Growing a New Tail* (Arlen House, 2015). Lisa's honours include the Hugo House New Works Fiction Award in 2015, Pushcart nominations in poetry and fiction, a 2021 Best-of-the-Net nomination, the Elizabeth Shanley Gerson Lecture in Irish Literature at University of Connecticut in 2011, with Geraldine Mills, a SURDNA Arts Teaching Fellowship, and American Association of University Professors (AAUP) writing related travel grants.

Lisa holds an MFA in Creative Writing from Stonecoast Creative Writing Program at University of Southern Maine. She teaches writing workshops online. She was recently awarded a Colorado Creative Industries and National Endowment for the Arts grant to provide poetry workshops for youth in 2022. She is a fiction editor for WORDPEACE (www.wordpeace.co), and a two-time mentor for Associated Writing Programs (AWP) W2W Program. Lisa organised and participated in events for the Milford Irish Heritage Society's Virtual Irish Arts Expo in 2020 and 2021, streaming Irish writers Geraldine Mills and Alan McMonagle. She lives in a small mountain town in Colorado but spends as much time as possible in Ireland.

www.lisactaylor.com
@dreamingchange